A
Variety
of
Verse
for
the Very Young

Chloe Frierson Fort

ILLUSTRATIONS BY

Dave Malone

ISBN 0-96263430-1

DEDICATION

To my Mother
who made all the hours shine

CONTENTS

CONVERSATION WITH A CREEK

Where do you think you're going,
You bubbling, tumbling creek?
With your rushing ripples of crystal
What is it that you seek?

I'm going to the sea, the salty sea,
The beautiful blue-green sea!
Where the spray dances high
And the sea gulls fly
And the tall waves welcome me!

I shall pass banks
All covered with moss,
I shall smooth pebbles
And give them a gloss!

Then on to the sea, the lilting sea,
The beautiful blue-green sea
Where the sky is wide
And the porpoises hide
And the white sand waits for me!

For though pleasant and lovely
My journey may be;
I must hurry and rush
Since waiting for me

There is the sea, the tossing sea,
The beautiful blue-green sea!
Where jewels are made in the spray
By the sun, and perhaps he may
Make beautiful jewels of me!

SPRINGTIME

Yellow sunshine has the spring for fingers
To coax young leaves from grey and empty boughs;
To gently lift the grass from soft brown earth
And tenderly unfold the petals of the flowers.

Since only mystic fingers such as these
Can to our earth such soft green beauty bring
Must we not know within our hearts
'Tis God Who gives the fingers to the spring?

DUSK

Across the lawn, over the grass
The evening shadows creep;
Drawing night behind them
So the earth can go to sleep.

WINTERTIME

Blow, wind, blow, beat upon the pane!
Play a tune upon my window
With your sharp staccato rain!

The wintry wind bends the trees
And tosses branches high,
Tracing shifting silhouettes
Against the wintry sky.

Now, some love best the Springtime,
And some the summer sun;
And some love autumn's flaming leaves
With crisp days just begun!

But only in the wintertime
The silvery shining ice appears
That coats the trees until they look
Like gleaming crystal chandeliers!

And Winter sends down drifting flakes
That turn the landscape white and still,
And make for splendid sledding
On every white and shining hill.

So with its snow and wind and rain,
I shall love the Winter best—
At least 'til Spring is here again!

SUNLIGHT AND SHADOW

Sunlight and shadow
On a dirt road—
Silver and gold
O'er a donkey and his load.

ME A FAIRY?

If I could be like a fairy
Behave the way that fairies do
I'd have such gay enchanting times
I think I'll tell you just a few.

I'd sail the seas in a silver ship,
Ride turquoise waves with a fringe of pearls
I'd lie in golden sun on a shore
Of golden sand in far-off worlds.

I'd fly on a leaf of bronze that's bright
Into a sky of mother-of-pearl,
Where I'd float on a cotton cloud of white
And then look down on a doll-house world.

Then I'd hold to a crystal raindrop
Falling swiftly through the air,
'Til I came to a blade of emerald grass
Then rest a bit, just sitting there.

And when the rainbow arches the sky
I'd climb to the top of its curve then slide
Right down its rows of sparkling gems
To the pot of gold on the other side!

Up with the silvery moon I'd climb
Far above the trees so high;
And then I'd cling to a silver star
In the deep, dark blue of the velvet sky!

Teakettle, teakettle, singing on the stove,
Tell me the song you sing!
Is it of cookies in a yellow jar
Or dough rolled out for some spicy thing?

Is it of woodsmoke blue and curling
In the early morning air
Or the smell of bacon cooking
That goes winding up the stair?

Is it your kitchen warm and cozy
When the winter's day is chill,
Yellow sunlight through the window,
Red geraniums on the sill?

THE TEAKETTLE SONG

Is it of kitty in the corner
Taking her lazy nap,
Or the stories Mother tells me
When I'm curled up in her lap?

Could it be of china dainty,
Sugary cakes to be served for tea,
Or door opened wide for Daddy
When he comes home to me?

Or do you sing because you're glad
To find yourself a part
Of a house that's filled with love and things
To warm a child's young heart?

DEAR MOON

Lovely golden moon
Floating through the sky–
Lovely golden moon
Hanging up so high!

Lovely yellow moon
Filling the night,
Warming my heart
With your lovely light!

You come riding from behind a cloud,
And over my blanket I peep at you.
I'm so glad to see you there!
Could you be glad to see me too?

THE LOCUST TREE

The old grey locust tree
In spring is very gay,
For the old grey locust tree
Is wearing a white bouquet!

TRAIN SONG

What says the clickety clack of the wheels?
What says the choo-choo when it blows?
Does it call for you to follow
To faraway places where the train track goes?

To cities with their buildings high
That stand and reach up to the sky;
And people, people with tramping feet
Beating a rhythm on sidewalk and street;
Where bells clang and horns blow
And lights say to stop and then to go?

Through deep green valleys with mighty trees;
Past sheep that graze on rolling leas;
Along streams that toss and tumble and leap,
Or by lazy rivers, slow and deep;
Through golden desert where cactus grows
Or mountains high where the wild wind blows?

Through the Southland, the gentle place
Where trees are hung with moss like lace;
Or in the North where snowy winds bite,
And the world is a world of crystal and white;
All over the land, uphill and down,
Through the whole country, round and round?

Or could the long-drawn whistle's wail
Say 'tis better far to have a home
Where love and friends and cheer are yours,
For 'tis lonely to forever roam!

OCTOBER

October steps across my lawn
With golden-winged feet,
And flings her green-gold scarf
Across the grass.

October scatters her leaves
Like red and golden coins
With every passing breeze.

She lets us know
The lush days of summer are going,
And chilly winter winds
Will soon be blowing.

But no one wants to say good-bye
To October's bright blue sky!

COUNTRY CHILLUN

Little country chillun
Wavin' at a train!
It'll take your dreams a-ridin'
And bring them back again!

THOUGHTS

What are little girls' thoughts of?
Perfume and powder and ribbons and lace—
Getting doll-baby fed and given a bath
And put to sleep in a cozy place.

"I shall wear dancing dresses" they say,
"And I shall put flowers in my hair.
My dolly's going to a party to-day
And pink is what she'll wear."

What are little boys' thoughts of?
Plants that grow and a hoe and a rake;
Old radio tubes and lots of screws
And construction plans of what he'll make.

He runs in saying, "There's a squash on the vine!
And the beans are ready to eat, come see!
I fixed the spray; it's working fine.
And I've found a new nest in the hackberry tree!"

MARCH WIND

The March wind snatches our voices
And carries them all away;
No wonder the old March wind
Has such a lot to say!

FIREFLIES

When the deep green
Of twilight comes,
Pricked by the golden glow
Of the fireflies' lanterns.

Who do you suppose they light
The way for?
Who do you suppose
Follows where they lead?

SNOWFLAKES

Let's talk about snowflakes
And how beautiful they are;

As pretty as a pearl,
As pretty as a star!
And let's remember
How different they are!
Let's remember
What care God takes
With each lacey flake He makes.
The one He puts on a rooftop,
The one on a shiny red sled;
The one on the woolen scarf
You wear around your head;
Each one is different
From each one under your snowman's hat.
Now what do you think of that?

CLOUD THINGS

To lie on my back and chew on grass
And watch the clouds go drifting past
That's what I love to do!
To feel a breeze across my face,
To feel the cool of a shady place—
I think you'd like it too!

Some clouds are like fleecy sheep
Grazing in a soft blue lea,
And some like sailboats all adrift
On an azure, curving sea.

But some look like big polar bears
And some are shaped like Christmas trees;
Some are like puppies with floppy ears
Or a slipper dancing on a breeze.

So when there's nothing much to do
Just lie on your back, half close your eyes
And I think that soon you'll see
You can find most anything in the skies!

AUTUMN

The autumn days have come,
The tawny days of Indian summer.
The amber air stands quiet,
As still as tea in a cup.

Lazy, hazy, autumn sun,
Could it be you've gotten tired?
You've shone so bright all summer,
Scarcely rested behind a cloud.

DAYDREAMS

What are daydreams made of?
Daydreams are made of wishes
Wishes of what we want to be
Wishes of what we want to see.

If we hold good and tight
To our wishes,
Try hard at what we want to be and do
Then someday our
Daydream wishes will all come true.

FAVORITE SOUNDS

These are some of my favorite sounds:
The cheerful crackling of flaming logs
Above a cozy hearth,
The lullaby patter of rain on the roof,
The gentle rippling of a stream,
The fresh sound of a rooster's crow at dawn,
The sweet notes of a mockingbird's song,
The rhythmic chorus of the night sounds of summer,
The soft whisper of a breeze in the leaves;
But the sweetest sounds of all must be
The words that say somebody loves me.

BUTTERCUP

I saw a golden buttercup
Shining in the golden sun.
I knew my life would golden be
'Til all its golden course was run!

DANDELION

Dandelion, dandelion
Gleaming like a star!
You are such an earthy thing
No one wonders what you are!

SECRET PLACE

I love a mossy, shady place
Green and quiet
With little white stars of Bethlehem
Blooming, and purple violets peeping
From underneath old bits of wood
Made grey by rain and wind and time.

Elves live here, I think,
And fairies and
All sorts of woodsy creatures.

If we listen really well,
We might hear secrets they can tell.